C is for Car

a vehicular alphabet book

Co-Written & Illustrated by: **Scott Park**
Co-Written & Edited by: **Glenn Oyoung**

Scott

To A. and E.: Don't tell mom I showed you what a handbrake turn was. Shhhhh!

Glenn

To J. and C., my two little gear heads. I can't wait to teach you girls how to drive stick and change your own tires.

A is for American

What's as American as baseball and apple pie?
Stock cars trading paint on a racetrack, that's what!

B is for British

A sleek roadster in British Racing Green is the way to tour the English countryside in style.

C is for
Cobra

It's the Shelby Cobra! It isn't a snake, but this winning little roadster sure knows how to bite the competition.

D is for Dragster

Buckle up! When the light turns green, it's time for launch!

E is for
Eighties

The 1980's. Cool cars, big hair and gullwing doors.

F is for French

Do the French love elegant styling? *Mais, oui!*

G is for German

Sporty cars with awesome handling make us say *danke schoen* to the Germans.

H is for
Hot Rod

Fixing up an old car and making it fast and cool has been a pastime for (older) kids like you for many years.

I is for
Italian

We love Italy – home to pizza, spaghetti, and beautiful red cars.
Che bello!

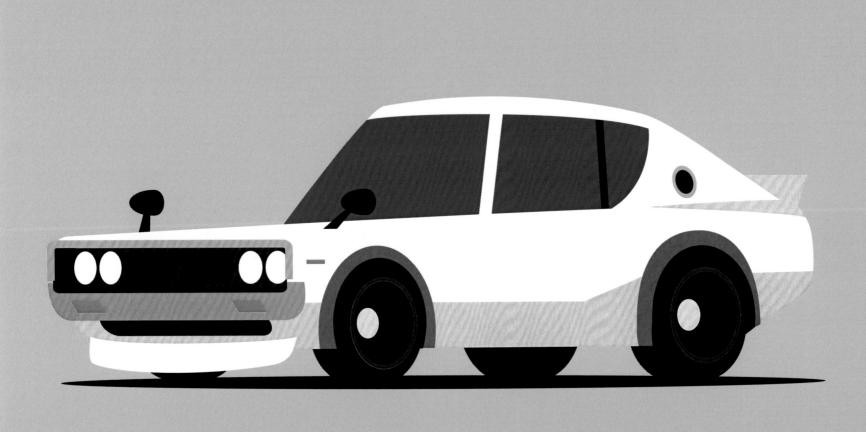

J is for Japanese

The land of the rising sun is home to small cars with big hearts!

K is for Kustom

We love special hot rods with snazzy paint designs and cool "kustom" parts.

L is for Lowrider

Super low and super cool, lowriders can raise eyebrows when they lift up each corner!

M is for Muscle Car

The 1970's were a time when cars had so much horsepower that we said they had muscles.

N is for Nitro

Nitrous or "nitro" is a kind of gas that makes cars so super fast! Hold on!

O is for
Off-Road

Off-roading in a raised truck or SUV is the way to get around rocks and through streams. What an adventure!

P is for Police Car

Police officers keep us safe from the bad guys, and they count on their trusty police cars to help them get around town. If you see the red and blue lights, move over!

Q is for Queenly

The stately British sedans are so comfortable; it's like riding on a cloud. That's the kind of ride that's fit for the Queen!

R is for Race Car

Race cars have neat paint jobs and they go really fast, especially the ones that race for Gulf. Smart gearheads know, there's no faster colors than Gulf Racing's famous orange and blue.

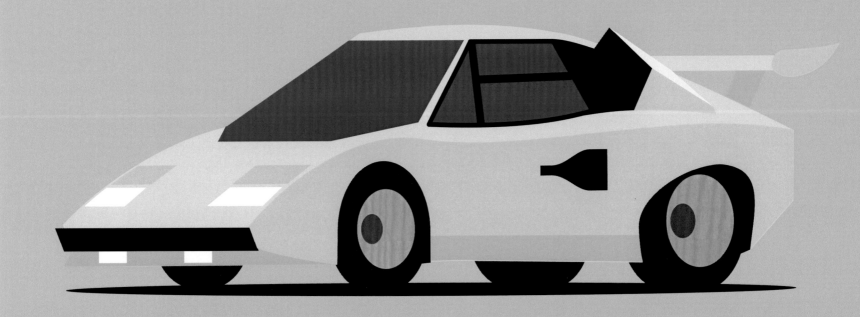

S is for Supercar

What makes a car a super car? It needs to look as fast as it is, standing still.

T is for Tailfins

In the 1950's the bigger the tailfin, the better!

U is for Used

You can save a lot of money and get a great car when you buy it used. It's like sharing, with cars.

V is for Van

In the 1970's and 1980's having a cool van with shag carpeting was all the rage. Bonus points for having a viking on the side.

W is for Woodie

Did you know that some cars were built with real wood on the sides?

48

X is for eXperimental

Experimental cars are ones that designers build to try and push their creativity. Often the things they learn are used on cars you can buy at the dealership.

TAXI

RATES
$1.00 FIRST ¼ MILE
15¢ EACH ADDITIONAL ¼ MILE

Y is for
Yellow Taxi

When you're in the big city and you need to go somewhere, you might hail a taxi to take you to your destination.

Z is for Z-Car

This car is so fast, it ended the book. It's time to catch some Zzzzzzzz's you little gear head, good night!

About Scott Park

Scott is an illustrator and advertising creative director, who lives in Toronto, Canada with his wife and kids. He's had a life long passion for cars, movies and spaceships. When he's not drawing obsessively geeky little pictures, he's teaching his kids about the important things in life. Like, cars, movies and spaceships.

About Glenn Oyoung

Glenn is a marketer and entrepreneur, who lives in Los Angeles with his wife and daughters (who he is encouraging to be little gear heads). He's loved playing with cars, drawing cars, and driving cars all his life, thanks to his mom Linda who took him to look at a freeway when he was a baby gearhead. When cars become silent and are driven by robots, Glenn and Scott will be at a track, schooling youngsters on how to drive stick.